ALONG THE WAY

Along the Way
To A Meeting Place
Copyright © 2025 by Jeffrey Aquino

Additional copies may be ordered from the publisher for educational,
business, promotional or premium use.
For information, contact ALIVE Book Publishing at:
alivebookpublishing.com, or call (925) 837-7303.

Book Design By Alex P. Johnson

ISBN 13
978-1-63132-271-6

Library of Congress Control Number: 2025924907

Library of Congress Cataloging-in-Publication Data
is available upon request.

First Edition

Published in the United States of America by ALIVE Book Publishing
an imprint of Advanced Publishing LLC
3200 A Danville Blvd., Suite 204, Alamo, California 94507
alivebookpublishing.com

PRINTED IN THE UNITED STATES OF AMERICA

10 9 8 7 6 5 4 3 2 1

ALONG THE WAY

TO A MEETING PLACE

JEFFREY AQUINO

ABOOKS

Alive Book Publishing

"Faith is the pencil of the soul that pictures heavenly things."
—T. Burbridge

To my beloved parents, Trinidad Mills Gaerlan Aquino and Jose M. Aquino, thank you for teaching me to always strive for excellence and to believe in myself, guided by God's love. And to my dear wife, Dale, who never seeks accolades, thank you for your incredible wisdom, patience, and support.

CONTENTS

ACKNOWLEDGMENTS

I want to begin by thanking Jesus Christ, the Blessed Virgin Mary, and the Apostles. With God's help, they have all given me the courage and strength to face life's challenges.

Speaking of challenges, I've always wondered about the trials my ancestors faced during their journeys across the world. I can only imagine their adventures, struggles, sorrows, and joys. I honor their stories. Now, I want to thank those who have supported and accompanied me along the way. First, I want to praise and honor my late parents, Trinidad and Jose Aquino, who continue to encourage me through the loving dreams they send. My cousin, Deanna DelaCruz, whom I affectionately call Auntie and confidant, has always shown interest in and faith in my writing. Before my beloved sister, Myrna Acosta, passed away, she also gave me the motivation to pursue writing when she acknowledged the beauty of my tribute given to our dear mother at her memorial. And, my cousin, Dr. Alvin Gaerlan, whose life story of our paternal grandfather, "The Almighty Moves Mountains," gave me the push to write my own story. And although my siblings, Ellen, Glenna, and my twin brother, Jethro, are distant, they will always remain close to my heart.

I also want to thank my close friend, Bob McEachran, for his friendship and interest in "Along the Way," as well as for introducing me to Eric Johnson and his wife, Peggy, from Alive Book Publishing. Thank you, Bob, Eric, and Peggy, for believing in my efforts. I am also grateful to Lorrie and Gary Timmons, who kindly allowed me to use the photographs included in my story, as they help bring it to life with illuminating images.

And finally, I can't forget those who always stand by me — my best friends: Zoe, my dog, and Gabriel, my cat. Both of them proofread my work during the early morning hours while I sip my coffee. Thanks, buddies!

PART ONE

INTRODUCTION

A Meeting Place

Growing up, I often heard my mother and grandmother praying in Castilian Spanish and my father reciting the Angelus. I only understood words like Jesus, Ave Maria, and Dios. I remember stories of my Igorot great-grandmother attending public gatherings dressed in long sleeves to hide her tattoos, which displayed her native Igorot heritage that she was embarrassed to show. These childhood memories have stayed with me over the years and now inspire me to explore my heritage. Who is better to learn from than my ancestors? From ancient visions and tribal customs to the Ten Commandments and voyages beyond, I humbly recognize that I am a meeting place of all that has come before.

CHAPTER ONE

God's Promise

This is a story of a quest, survival, and affirmation. For years, I have researched my family's origins, and now I am returning to the roots of my ancestors. The journey will be challenging, but my faith in God will sustain me. I need to prepare; there's still much to learn. But my eyes are heavy, and I must rest now...

Startled, I woke up to a roar and a flash of bright light outside my window. I opened the shade to see a beautiful landscape with peaceful clouds, a rainbow, and a vast sea stretching across the horizon. It was so calm, like floating in heaven, looking down on God's final day of creation. I rubbed my eyes and blinked; the vision disappeared. Was it a mirage?

I stepped outside, unsure of what I would find, and looked up at the sky. A ray of light shone over a shimmering sea, with waves crashing onto the shore. A white bird soared above the water. I heard chirps, clucks, squeals, howls, grunts, and roars. A large wooden plank floated along the shoreline. Could it have come from an ancient ark walkway trodden by animals, two of a kind? I became captivated by the scene, and as I stared at it, the vision faded.

I was confused and needed to understand these fleeting visions. Then God revealed the answer to me: through these visions, God sent me a message that He is an eternal presence in the world He created. It was then that I realized God would always be with me, no matter what I face. "So do not fear, for I am with you; do not be dismayed, for I am your God. I will strengthen you and help you; I will uphold you with my righteous right hand (Isaiah 41:10)."

CHAPTER TWO

The Apostles

Guided by God's promise, I prepared for my quest. I looked up at the sky with confidence and began my journey, carrying only a knapsack and a Bible. I hiked across the desolate landscape for hours. It was hot, and the intense heat drained my strength. I searched for shelter and found a cave. The cave's entrance was intimidating. I ran a stick around the entrance to ward off spiders, snakes, or bats, then cautiously entered the cave, praying, Jesus, I trust in you. "Yea, though I walk through the valley of the shadow of death, I will fear no evil: for thou art with me; thy rod and staff they comfort me (Psalm 23:4)." Even in the darkest and most difficult times, God's presence and protection are enough to overcome fear. With this affirmation, I pressed further into the cave.

Probing the depths of the cave was exciting, but I shivered from the constant cold. I wondered, "Did cavemen catch colds?" To warm up, I dug a hole in the cave's floor, crawled into it, and lay down. As I rested there, I thought of God's hands wrapping around me. I felt the warmth of His hands as my bedding, and I peacefully slept through the night.

When I woke up the next day, I felt peaceful but longed for companions to share my journey. Throughout the cave, rocks were plentiful. I collected twelve rocks and named each after one of Jesus's Twelve Apostles. Using a sharp stone, I etched each rock's initials and the Sign of the Cross into them. Jesus's apostles were ordinary men from different backgrounds, whom Jesus chose to spread His message: Simon Peter, Andrew, James the son of Zebedee, James the son of Alphaeus, John, Philip, Bartholomew, Thomas, Matthew, Thaddeus, Simon the Zealot, and Judas Iscariot. These men were chosen as personal witnesses to testify to the truth of the good news about Jesus's life and resurrection. With my rock apostles nearby, I knelt and prayed. I felt at peace; my apostles brought me comfort and spiritual nourishment.

Soon, however, my stomach began to rumble with hunger. I thought of my wife and how we always pray together before meals. I cherished this memory, but my grumbling stomach reminded me that speed was crucial for survival. I resumed my search for food as hunger heightened my senses. I was upset by the idea of only imagining food I couldn't taste, smell, or touch. Despite this torment, my hunt for food took me deeper into the cave, where I stepped into a puddle of foul, muddy water. I dared not touch or drink from it, fearing contamination from bats.

Undeterred by the muddy puddle, I kept searching. From studying survival manuals, I've learned that shrimp, fish, crabs, and snails live in aquatic environments inside caves. There are also beetles, cave crickets, ticks, worms, and scorpions. Plants can grow in the twilight areas of caves where sunlight filters. However, in the darkness of this cave, I couldn't find my way. I was as blind as a bat.

Not wanting to risk injury while stumbling through the cave's darkness, I abandoned my plan to eat insects. I sat down in dismay on the cold cave floor, pulling my knees to my chest. As I sat there, I heard a faint dripping. I reached down and felt moisture on the cave floor. I licked my fingers; there was no foul odor or taste. It was water! My excitement brought tears to my eyes. Turning onto my knees and pressing my hands to the cave wall, I prayed. I felt joy and inner peace as I imagined touching Jesus's feet on the crucifix, as Jesus offers my body and soul salvation.

Energized by my faith and the discovery of water, I weighed my options: go deeper into the cave or head outside to find food. Drawn to the outside light, I climbed back to the cave's entrance. As I waved goodbye to my apostle rocks, I reflected on a biblical verse where Jesus spoke to His Twelve Apostles, "A little while, and you will see me no more; and then there after a little while you will see me. (John 16:16)." Jesus also told the disciples to be of good cheer and that "inner peace and courage amid tribulation could only be experienced by abiding by Him (John 2:28)." As I made my way to the cave's entrance, I knew my faith in Christ would be tested with more challenges. But I was prepared with Christ's promise and the teachings of the Apostles.

CHAPTER THREE

I Am Not Alone

While exploring outside for food, I found dandelions, wild leeks, and berries. I picked a dandelion, which is a good source of fiber. It had a bitter taste with a slight touch of sweetness. To add more variety, I also found some leeks and berries. It was a satisfying meal, and I digested everything easily without any noticeable problems, just occasional burps.

From my scouting days, I remembered that protein is essential for a balanced diet. I also recalled how to set traps and start a campfire. I collected leaves and twigs for tinder, then found some smooth, glossy stones to use as a base for the fire. I also gathered some large sticks to build a trap. It had been a while since I practiced my survival skills, but I had plenty of time to test them out. I set up a small trap away from the campsite and then built a fire. I struck rocks together at different angles, and surprisingly, sparks flew. I hit the rocks again directly over the pile of leaves and twigs, creating sparks that eventually ignited a glowing fire.

As the fire burned, I checked my trap. I had caught my dinner. With this blessing from God, I cried, made the Sign of the Cross, and prayed, "Bless us, Lord, and these Thy gifts, which we are to receive from Thy Bounty. Through Christ our Lord. Amen."

My dinner refreshed me, boosting my eagerness to continue my journey. There was much to learn, and I was an enthusiastic student. As I hiked along, I followed a narrow, winding crevice in the ground. I guessed that this crevice might be the remains of a once-flowing stream. I picked up a stick and dug about six inches into the crevice. The ground was cool and moist. I pushed the stick deeper into the soil, and water burst up to the surface. I wiped my face with the cool water and drank. God is good!

It had been a day full of discoveries and blessings, and I was ready to sleep. I made a bed with leaves and twigs for my mattress and used my knapsack as a pillow. As I lay there in thought, I looked up at the sky, which was filled with countless stars shining down on me. I welcomed the symphony of sounds around me: animals calling, leaves rustling, and tree branches snapping under the weight of nocturnal creatures on the hunt. The sights and sounds of God's creation reassured me that I was not alone.

CHAPTER FOUR

My Rebirth

At dawn, my peaceful sleep was disrupted by the buzzing of insects crawling over my face. I swatted at the intruders with my knapsack as I hurried back to the cave's sanctuary and my apostle rocks. However, our reunion was suddenly interrupted; I was thrown to the ground by the intense shaking of the cave, accompanied by a thunderous boom that echoed throughout.

With the cave crumbling around me, I cried out, "My God, is this going to be my Last Supper?" I was confronted with an abyss of darkness, where despair could easily take over me. I looked toward the cave's entrance, and through the rubble, I saw a sliver of light shining from a small hole. I crawled toward the light and cried out, "This cave will not be my tomb!"

I turned to Jesus and called for help. He sent me back to my apostle rocks, where I gathered them close, gaining strength and calm. When the shaking in the cave stopped, I collected my apostle rocks and put them in my knapsack. I looked at the light shining from the small hole, and clutching my knapsack, I pulled myself through the cave's debris.

When I reached the hole, I took a deep breath; the fresh air was invigorating. Then, with all my strength, I pushed a boulder partially blocking my path. Nothing budged. Feeling faint and with aching muscles, I groaned loudly and tried again. The boulder shifted, creating enough space for me to feel the air rush over my face. With my heart pounding, I cleared away the debris, freeing my head. Ignoring the pain, I gave one final push with my shoulders and widened the hole. Jerking my body from side to side, I crawled out of the cave, still clutching my knapsack, into the bright light and fresh air. I cried out as if I were emerging from my mother's womb. Was this my rebirth into a new world of mysteries and visions?

I was pulled back to the image of the narrow cleft where an old stream might have once flowed. Was that discovery a coincidence, a divine sign, or a test of faith? I took it as a message from God to follow the path He laid out.

And with my apostles, my journey continued.

CHAPTER FIVE

Casting My Net

I decided to return to the narrow cleft and follow its path to see where it might lead. The afternoon was hot, and my mouth was dry. The stick I had pushed into the cleft in search of water still stood upright, like a sundial; its shadow pointed to noon. Water seeped up from the ground at the base of the stick. I scooped some mud with my handkerchief and squeezed it over my mouth, revealing drops of gritty, pungent water that were barely wet enough to quench my thirst. Despite its unusual taste and texture, I drank gritty water.

I figured that the cleft was once a stream fed by an underground spring, so I kept walking along its path, searching for more water and some food. I found flowers and herbs; they would make a good salad. I pulled a handful of plants from the ground, their roots dripping with fresh water. With this discovery of clean water, I packed the plants into my knapsack and continued looking for more water.

Throughout the cleft, there were moist holes where animals might have dug in search of insects and water. Like the animals that passed this way before me, I also needed sustenance. I prayed, asking for Jesus's help. My prayers were answered as I looked up at the sky. There was a cloud shaped like a tall cactus. The arm of the cactus seemed to point directly at me, suggesting I pay closer attention to my surroundings. I remembered a Bible passage where Jesus told Peter the Fisherman to cast his empty net into deeper water. When Peter pulled up his net, it was full of fish. So, as Peter did, I looked "deeper" and followed Jesus's guidance given through the image of the cactus-shaped cloud. Becoming more observant, I walked further along the cleft and then sat down to rest. I must have dozed off because when I raised my head, I saw a lone, tall cactus not far in the distance. I jumped up, ran to it, and fell flat on my chest at its base. Using my bare hands and a stick, I dug around the base and then poked a hole near the primary root with a sharp stone. Pure, clean water began to seep out, and I drank eagerly, replenishing my bodily fluids. Thank You, Jesus! Rejuvenated, I returned to the cleft, taking rest stops along the way and offering prayers of gratitude for all the blessings I had received during my journey.

As sundown neared, I decided to stop for the night when I saw a small, pointed shape peeking out from the cleft. Using the full moon as my light, I reached down and pulled it out. It looked like a rusty blade from a Bowie knife, missing its handle and measuring approximately sixteen inches in length. This blade could be a helpful tool. It was time to call it a night.

I dropped my knapsack on the ground and started setting up my campsite. First, I needed to build a fire. To block the evening wind, I dug a shallow fire pit near an outcropping of rocks, placed some stones inside, and covered it with branches and twigs. Then, I held a rough stone over the fire pit and struck it with my Bowie knife, creating sparks that ignited the sticks and twigs. As the fire grew, I added more stones around it, where I roasted cactus and other plants. I ate lightly and prayed, thanking the Lord for my meal, provisions, and the beautiful day. As the fire died down, I threw dirt on it to extinguish the flames, then covered the warm stones with more soil to create a cozy bed. My sleep came quickly.

CHAPTER SIX
God's Plan

The next morning, cloudy skies greeted me. I started my day with a prayer, "Thank you, Jesus, for this new day. I look forward to a positive day with your Spirit walking by my side and along the way." With this prayer, I got up, grabbed my knapsack, and set out for the day's adventure.

As I hiked, I noticed a distant field of debris, remnants of past travelers who had passed through this way. I jogged over to the debris, which looked like the remains of a hastily abandoned campsite. There was plenty to scavenge: a torn tent, a duffel bag, a heavy backpack, an empty canteen, and a nylon pouch holding seasoning packets, soap, gloves, and towels. I quickly packed the duffel bag with my finds and my knapsack, then slung it over my shoulder. I laughed and cried, struck by the irony of having an empty canteen while still feeling thirsty. Yet, my resolve grew stronger as I remembered God's promise, "The Lord is close to the brokenhearted and saves those who are crushed in spirit (Psalm 34:18)." I praised God and thanked Him for His guidance and comfort. Filled with renewed strength from God's words, I continued my journey.

As I resumed my hike, a foul smell surrounded me—my body odor. I could almost taste the stench, which resembled a decayed, dead animal. I wondered if I would attract a beast or scare it away. Perhaps I would become the Flavor of the Month. My urge to clean myself became urgent. Suddenly, the overcast clouds parted, and raindrops fell on my arm, followed by heavy rain. The dry cleft transformed into a rushing stream—a sign of God's power that sustains and purifies all life. I raised my open canteen toward the sky, filling it with the precious rainwater, and then drank, giving thanks to God's glory.

As the rain continued to fall, I took off my clothes and left them on the ground. I found a bar of soap in the salvaged duffel bag and scrubbed every part of my body. Then, I washed my clothes, wrung them out, and hung them on some bushes to dry.

By sunset, the rain had stopped, so I put on my clean clothes and prepared for the night. The poncho and the torn nylon tent I had scavenged would serve as my blankets. I huddled under a bush. It was cold, but I stayed warm by jogging in place periodically to circulate my blood. As I jogged, my thoughts drifted back to my school days and the lessons I had learned. I focused on a specific lesson about God's divine nature and His plan for humanity.

First, the Restoration between humanity and God results from the fall of Adam and Eve, allowing humanity to be saved from sin and gain access to God. Second, Salvation and Eternal Life offer forgiveness of sins and the promise of eternal life both now and in the future, with the hope of a forever relationship with God. Third, there are Individual Purposes; these personal plans help people fulfill their unique roles and contribute to God's larger plans. Additionally, there is a biblical reference to "spread your seeds," which highlights the importance of maintaining the family line by having many children. God promises Abraham, "I will surely bless you, and I will multiply your offspring as the stars of heaven and as the sand that is on the seashore (Genesis 22:17)."

And finally, an example of God's Plan in action can be seen as it unfolds through individuals and throughout history. For instance, the story of Noah and the Ark or the calling of Abraham shows how God's plan aims to restore His relationship with humanity.

With God's plan in my arsenal, I felt reassured and stronger. When I woke up the next morning, I felt queasy, but I was determined to face the day's challenges. I experienced dry heaves followed by severe nausea. I had eaten plenty of plants the night before, and I believed that the rainwater I drank would help detoxify my body. I remembered a passage from the Bible where Jesus sent the Apostles to preach the Gospel and heal the sick. So, with Jesus as my healer and my knapsack of apostle rocks as my pillow, I lay on the ground and prayed for healing. I knew that God's divine healing would come either now or in the Ultimate Healing in Heaven. I became emotional, trusting in Jesus, knowing that my physical healing and spiritual well-being come from Him. I drank some water, and as I gained strength, I envisioned God's marvelous creation: "The heavens declare the glory of God, and the sky above proclaims His handiwork (Psalm 19:1)." The greatness of God is ever-present. The fact that the universe began is something we can observe by looking at the heavens and sky.

We are God's handiwork. Furthermore, a person needs faith and the Bible to have a proper relationship with God. And one only needs to look inside to realize the existence of God.

CHAPTER SEVEN

The Rosary

With my spirituality renewed, I regained my physical strength. Before starting my trek again, I checked the duffel bag, which contained items I had quickly gathered from the abandoned campsite. I was pleased with what I had scavenged: various kitchen utensils, a black-handled Swiss knife, and a backpack holding other miscellaneous items. I was eager to begin my day's hike, so I tossed my knapsack and the canteen into the duffel bag, zipped it up, and hoisted it over my shoulder. The misty morning was so refreshing. I felt good and was satisfied with my provisions and the full canteen. But I knew I still had to continue my food search. May the Lord be with me. Talking with God is so gratifying.

I maintained a steady pace while hiking for about an hour, then began jogging until my legs cramped. I slowed down, whistled, and hummed a tune as I continued. After a while, I paused for a break and took a drink of water. Using practicality and good judgment, I watched my heart rate and stress levels while conserving the water in my canteen.

I shifted my thoughts back to food. In the duffel bag, I found a frying pan. Now that I could cook a meal properly, I continued searching for food. I discovered a variety of crickets, grasshoppers, and other insects. I gathered as many as I could, stuffing them into my spare socks. I built a campfire, boiled some water in my frying pan, and then tossed in a few grasshoppers. As the water boiled away, an oily residue remained along with the crispy grasshoppers, to which I added some salt from my supplies. My first pan-fried meal would not only be tasty but also healthy. I made the Sign of the Cross with my prayer, giving thanks for the Lord's provision and recognizing Him as the source of all blessings.

With my stomach full, I was ready for bed. I took a sip of water and wrapped myself in the poncho and torn tent. I lay on the ground, sang a hymn, and recited an evening prayer: "Dear Lord, as the day ends, thank you for your blessings. Grant me peace as I rest and protect me through the night. Amen." I closed my eyes, and my muscles relaxed as I remembered wonderful family moments. My sleep must have been long and deep; I woke up the next morning feeling calm, energized, and focused. I sat up, reached into my pocket for my Rosary, and began to pray. Praying the Rosary helps me meditate on the life and events of Jesus and Mary and reflect on specific mysteries or moments. It's also my way of putting on the armor of God, serving as my shield and sword against unforeseen evil. It's like having a five-caliber spiritual machine gun because the names Jesus and Mary are repeated fifty times, making the Devil tremble in fear as he's pushed back to the netherworld while I stand firm in my faith in Jesus Christ.

When I finished the Rosary, I packed my gear. I began my hike with a renewed appreciation for the beauty and simplicity of God's creation: a flock of finches flying across the sky and a turtle digging at the edge of the flowing stream where only cracked, dry earth had been there before. I also saw a rabbit hopping along the stream and an antelope leaping through the landscape. Although these sights were simple, they lifted my spirits; I felt inspired. I looked ahead for more of God's demonstration of His love.

CHAPTER EIGHT

Glory

Along the way, in the distance, I saw a bend in the stream. I quickened my pace to reach the bend. The distance was deceptive; it felt like miles. When I finally reached the bend, I blinked and rubbed my eyes in disbelief. The narrow stream led me to a beautiful flowing river that signaled promising adventures.

I decided to make this riverbank oasis my next resting spot, so I took a nap. I must have slept for hours; I woke up ready to continue my trek with my duffel bag in tow. Along the riverbank, various trees grew, including birch and maple. These trees could provide material for a raft to carry me down the uncharted parts of the river. I used some riverbank sand and a rock to sharpen my Bowie knife to a razor-sharp edge. Then, I cut some tree branches and found thick vines on the riverbank. Along with the ropes I salvaged from the abandoned campsite, I had all the materials I needed to build my raft.

I chose to build my raft near the edge of the river because the finished raft would be too heavy for me to drag into the water. The raft needed to be a good size so it could carry my gear. It took some time to assemble, but it was well worth the effort. When I finished, I sat down and drank the remaining water from my canteen. Shipbuilding is such a strenuous yet rewarding job. Next, I prepared my provisions for the voyage, replenishing the canteen's water and boiling some bugs for snacks.

I named my raft 'Glory' after the Latin word 'Gloria,'

which is associated with praising God. I loaded my gear onto Glory and then christened her with a rock for good luck, just as you would traditionally christen a new ship with a champagne bottle. Then I shouted, "Glory," and with the prayer, "In the name of the Father, Son, and Holy Spirit. Amen," I made the Sign of the Cross with my right hand. The Sign of the Cross is a declaration of faith, a renewal of baptism, a symbol of discipleship, an acceptance of suffering, a shield against evil, and a victory over self-indulgence. It gives me confidence and strength. As I cast off into the unknown, I prayed, "I place my fate in your hands, Jesus, who art all good." Then I looked up at the mast I had made to represent the Holy Cross. Glory proudly flew a sail, the torn nylon tent catching winds sent from Heaven.

Finally, I could relax and let the river carry me wherever it wanted. I looked back wistfully at the land I was leaving and then looked ahead to new adventures. The flowing river's motion was soothing; I placed my head on my knapsack and drifted off to sleep. I don't know how long I slept, but I suddenly woke up, panicked, with my heart pounding. I had failed to anticipate where the river might take me. I had been preoccupied wondering what lay beyond the horizon. Would the river lead me to a larger body of water, like a lake, sea, ocean, or even civilization? To calm myself, I repeated Jesus' words, urging others to remain calm and hopeful, "Do not let your hearts be troubled. You believe in God, believe also in Me (John 14:1)."

The river quickened its flow and led into the sea. In the distance, land appeared, and Glory drifted with the current toward it. When Glory reached the shore, I jumped into the water, pulled her to safety, and then stepped onto dry ground. I saw no signs of life; this place seemed deserted.

As I looked out over the landscape, composed only of shrubs and stones, I thought of the biblical story of Moses and the Burning Bush in the wilderness. Flames did not consume the Burning Bush. Instead, God revealed His identity to Moses through the bush and chose him to lead the Israelites out of slavery and into Egypt. Although Moses initially hesitated, he eventually obeyed, trusting that God's presence and power would always protect and guide him.

I didn't see a Burning Bush in this new land, but the story taught me that God can reveal Himself and His purpose through ordinary things. And that, my faith, obedience, and trust in Him will sustain me.

CHAPTER NINE

The New Land

My first steps onto the new land were exciting, even joyful. It felt as if my parents and the Heavenly Father were watching me take my first step, ready to catch me if I fell. "And He shall direct your path (Proverbs 3:5,6)." Fortified by these words, I immediately set out to conquer the first obstacle confronting me—a ridge crowned by a tall obelisk, a sign of civilization. As I ascended the ridge, I heard voices speaking in unfamiliar languages coming from the obelisk. Was this the Tower of Babel? According to the Book of Genesis, God's destruction of the Tower of Babel is said to explain the origin of languages and cultures on Earth. Crowds of humans, in their arrogance, believed they were more powerful than God and could build a tower to reach Heaven. Yet, God destroyed the tower, scattering humankind and their many languages across the world.

As I climbed further up the ridge, I was met with a roar and a blinding flash as the obelisk exploded before my eyes. Rocks shifted beneath my feet, and I fell back, grabbing at plants and bushes to slow my descent. I cried out loudly, "God have mercy on me!" And as I tumbled down the ridge, I called out, "Mama!" My mother was always there for me when I was hurt, wiping away my tears.

Physically and emotionally battered, I reached the base of the ridge. Dazed and in pain, I ate the leaves I still held in my hand. Then I crawled back to the raft for my canteen. As I lay on the raft beneath the protection of my cross-shaped mast, my head throbbed. I slowly raised myself, drank some water, and dangled my feet over the edge of the raft. The cool water reminded me of how Jesus washed His disciples' feet with humility and mutual love, foreshadowing His ultimate act of servanthood — His death on the cross — and the spiritual cleansing He offers. Thank you, Jesus.

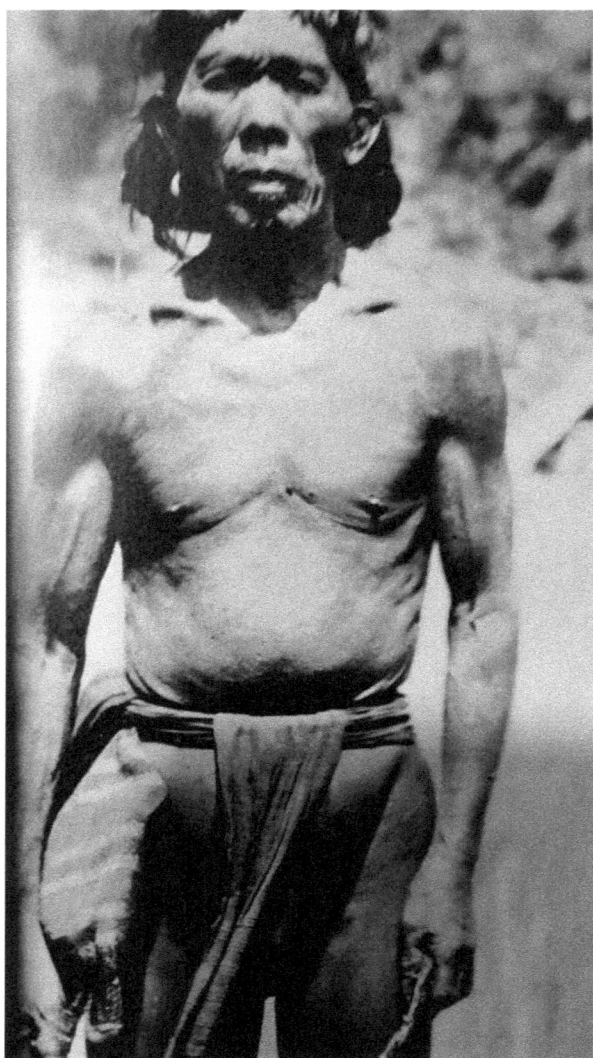

CHAPTER TEN

Visions

As I lay on the raft, my head throbbed. I closed my eyes and saw vividly colored lights flashing in the night sky, along with a full moon and shooting stars. I was soaring through the air, reaching out to touch a star, then falling onto a floating ice sheet that cracked and broke beneath me. I levitated above the melting ice. As I soared in the sky, I watched the rise and fall of the seas below.

Then, another flash of light; the vision of the seas disappears, replaced by dark figures making clicking sounds. I find myself among gorillas and orangutans, which mimic all my movements, reaching out to touch me. They pound grapes and drink juice. Other apes with a human-like appearance eat tree bark and leaves, then fall to the ground in a mummified state. Some offer food to the spirits on freshly dug graves and outcroppings of rock, where ghostly spirits are believed to celebrate their presence.

I closed my eyes and spun around dizzily. I saw short beings with sturdy features, bushy eyebrows, and broad noses. They are headhunters, grunting and dancing wildly with their hands flailing, celebrating their kill before retreating to their caves. With more flashes of light, I see tribesmen jumping into dugout canoes as rocks and spears fly overhead. Am I witnessing a cautionary tale of human evolution in progress?

The scene quickly shifts to an image of a tall man with slanted eyes leading battles in foreign lands. I feel fear, yet I am in awe of this warrior. Could this be Genghis Khan, a Mongolian ancestor? He leads dark figures riding on horse-

back, carrying spears and drawn swords, across the coun-
tryside, capturing tribeswomen as the spoils of war.

I shake my head and rub my eyes. My visions persist with
vivid detail. I see a native ancestor, an Igorot, a mountain
man, walking along a dirt road winding through the hills of
my homeland, the Philippines. He wears a bahag, a hand-
woven loincloth wrapped around his waist and tied between
his legs. The color and woven pattern of his loincloth indicate
his high social status. I learned about the Igorot from stories
my elders told me. They said that the Igorot are descendants
of humans who migrated from Africa to Southeast Asia,
crossing the oceans millions of years ago. My elders also
taught me that the Igorot faced discrimination, misconcep-
tions, and mistreatment by fellow 'lowland' Filipinos. The
Igorot were thought to be uncivilized and savage. Yet, I em-
brace the Igorot branch of my family tree, along with my
other ancestors: the Moors, the North African Berbers, the
Arabs, the Normans, the Vikings, and the Spaniards who
brought Catholicism to the Philippines.

CHAPTER ELEVEN

The Staircase

My visions of my ancient relatives fade into a haze, and I find myself in a room with a winding staircase. I wonder what might be at the top. I climb the steps, praying that each one will bring me closer to salvation. When I reach the top, I see a mirror, and as I peer into it, I am cautious about what it might reveal. Might I see only my physical self or a deeper awareness of my inner being? Might I see a reflection of my life, either filled with joy or marked by sorrow?

I did not get an answer. The mirror fogged up. My head ached, and I felt intense shaking. The lights flickered, and the hair on my arms stood up. I smelled the scent of flowers. Then I was wrapped in deep bliss, warm and comforting. This was peace and clarity, the breath of Everlasting Life. I am in communion with God through the consecrated body and blood of Christ. Glory to God in the Highest. Amen.

CHAPTER TWELVE

The Twelve

I hear a voice and feel myself pulled away from my visions, moving through space and time.

"Sir, sir, are you okay? Do you know where you are? Sir, wake up. Do you know where you are?" I wondered to myself, "Where are these voices coming from?" I looked up and groggily responded, "What, what? I don't know where I am, but I know where I've been."

I rubbed my head and opened my eyes. A doctor leaned over me and said, "You got quite a bump on your head when the plane hit turbulence. You've been out for quite a while. We've been trying to figure out who you are and where you came from. Tell me, are you an Arab, an East Indian, or a Spaniard?"

I answered, "All of these; I am Filipino. Have I been dreaming?" The doctor smiled and said, "Ah, the Philippines, the melting pot of Asia. You appear to be healthy and aware of your surroundings. I'm going to release you so you can resume your flight."

As I was getting ready to leave, a nurse entered the room to clear the area. I grabbed my luggage and headed toward the door. The nurse called out to me, "Sir, you forgot this." I turned back to her, and she handed me a worn, tattered knapsack. I opened it. Inside, there was a beautifully woven loincloth and some rocks. I counted twelve.

PART TWO

Crossing Paths

The rich histories of two very different landmasses—the Iberian Peninsula and the Philippines—have shaped my genetic identity. Currently, the Iberian Peninsula includes Spain, Portugal, Andorra, a small part of France, and Gibraltar. It is in southwestern Europe and is separated from the rest of the continent by the Pyrenees Mountains. The Philippines is an archipelagic country in Southeast Asia situated in the western Pacific Ocean, comprising 7,641 islands.

Imagine the mixing of all our ancestors' DNA, the molecule that carries genetic information for all living beings. In genetics, our ancestor genes—those passed down from previous generations—are combined with descendant genes—the genes inherited by future generations. These genes shape our heredity and ethnicity.

It's incredible how seafaring ancestors traveled across the Iberian Peninsula and the Philippine Archipelago to reach, conquer, and settle other lands. Many ethnic groups encountered each other along the way.

- Celts migrated from central Europe.
- Phoenicians – originated in the Levant (modern-day Lebanon, Israel, and Syria)
- Greeks inhabited mainland Greece and the Greek islands, establishing colonies along the Mediterranean coast.
- Carthaginians – Phoenician settlers who established the city of Carthage in North Africa. They came from Tyre, a city in Phoenicia located on the eastern Mediterranean coast.

- Romans—comprising Latins and Sabines who came from the city of Rome in Latium, central Italy—conquered the Iberian Peninsula (modern-day Spain and Portugal), establishing the Roman Empire.
- Germanic tribes – originated in an area that includes today's Scandinavia, Denmark, and northern Germany.
- Moors – North African Muslims of mixed Arab, Spanish, and Berber origins invaded Iberia in 711.
- Viking Raids – Vikings launched incursions into the Iberian Peninsula, attacking coastal cities.
- Sephardic Jews—originally from Iberia, which includes Spain and Portugal—established communities across North Africa, the Middle East, and Europe. Many of them live in Israel today.
- Austronesian roots: originating from the original inhabitants and migrations from Taiwan. The Austronesian peoples comprise a large group of ethnolinguistic communities that inhabit a wide geographic area, including Taiwan, Maritime Southeast Asia, parts of mainland Southeast Asia, Micronesia, coastal New Guinea, Island Melanesia, Polynesia, and Madagascar.
- Chinese migrants and other East Asian influences

With this mix of ethnic groups, the idea of my being a "100% pure Filipino" has no scientific basis. This was confirmed by a DNA test, which showed that I am only 49.1% Filipino. My genetic background is a result of centuries of migration, intermarriage, and cultural exchange with various peoples, not only in Iberia but also in the Philippines. The Philippines, often referred to as the "Melting Pot of Asia," has a rich history of migration and cultural exchange that has created a unique genetic blend.

CONCLUSION

So, here we are—has my story ended? My journey continues as I seek a deeper connection with my heritage and expand my understanding of it. My research, visions, and especially my spiritual affirmations have guided me on a path of self-reflection and discovery. It has been demanding but rewarding. For that, I am grateful for everything I have experienced along the way.

BIBLIOGRAPHY

Adams, Robert I. (2022 - 2024). *Revelation Revealed: Uncovering What the Last Book in the Bible Says About the Last Day.* Kindle Direct Publishing

Fletcher, Richard. (1992). *Moorish Spain.* University of California Press, Berkeley and Los Angeles, California

Phillips, Rod. (2000*). A Short History of Wine.* HarperCollins Publishers Inc.

Pigafetta, Antonio. (1522). *The First Voyage Around the World: An Account of Magellan's Expedition.* Bibl. Ambrosiana, L.103 Sup., Milan, Italy. edited by Theodore J. Cachey, Jr. (1995). Marsilio Publishers, New York, NY.

Pringle, Heather (2000). *The Mummy Congress: Science, Obsession, and the Everlasting Dead.* Hyperion

The New American Bible, revised edition 2011 by Catholic Book Publishing Corp., N.J.

Wikipedia contributors. (2025, July 11). Culture of the Philippines. In *Wikipedia, The Free Encyclopedia.* Retrieved 01:13, July 22, 2025, from https://en.wikipedia.org/w/index.php?title=Culture_of_the_Philippines&oldid=1299950813

Wikipedia contributors, 'Genetic history of the Iberian Peninsula', *Wikipedia, The Free Encyclopedia,* 17 July 2025, 22:31 UTC, <https://en.wikipedia.org/w/index.php?title=Genetic_history_of_the_Iberian_Peninsula&oldid=1301064924> [accessed 22 July 2025]

ABOOKS

ALIVE Book Publishing and ALIVE Publishing Group
are imprints of Advanced Publishing LLC,
3200 A Danville Blvd., Suite 204, Alamo, California 94507

Telephone: 925.837.7303
alivebookpublishing.com

www.ingramcontent.com/pod-product-compliance
Lightning Source LLC
LaVergne TN
LVHW010306070426
835509LV00024B/3483